Addiction

PLAIN AND SIMPLE

AN INTIMATE JOURNEY INTO THE WORLD OF AN ADDICT

DR. DEBORAH DAY AIKENS

ISBN: 1475190107
ISBN 13: 9781475190106

ACKNOWLEDGMENTS

With grace and humility, I pay homage to my Higher Power from which all things are possible.

To the memory of my grandfather, Frederick C. Ferguson, who empowered me with the light of knowledge.

To my parents and grandparents, who instilled in me a sense of security and perseverance.

To my spiritual soul mate: my best friend, my husband, and to our children who remind me everyday, just how blessed I am.

To all of the sick and suffering addicts, remember the passage: "I once was lost and now am found." (Amazing Grace)

Remember you are God's child.

Listen to the voices of thousands of addicts

Not all

But all shall remain anonymous

As I live and breathe, I will here and forever more,

champion the struggle and the challenges of addiction

As well as the power and miracle of recovery

I Am God's Child

If you want to know who I am, put down all of those books that spout theories about all addicts. The assertion, in and of itself, is insulting.

I am not many, I am one.

I am God's child just like you.

I am a seed unsown, or a flower unbloomed, succumb by the elements.

I didn't start out as an addict; I never wanted to be an addict.

But somewhere, somehow, I got lost:

Like Alice, who "fell down the rabbit hole," or Dorothy who couldn't find her way home.

I got caught up in the grips of addiction, and I can't get out.

Everyday, I yell for help, but you don't hear me: "Hell," you don't even see me. All you see is an addict: A wasted, worthless being, which you conveniently ignore; that you would rather do without.

Stop and listen to me.

I use because I can; that is what is available to me.

I use because it used to be fun using.

I use because I'm hurt.

I use because I don't know what else to do.

I use because if I don't, I will be sick.

I am God's child: A human just like you.

But I am lost in my own contained world called, "Self."

I live under the illusion of control, but I am powerless.

If you want to understand who I am; listen to me, respect me, have some compassion for me, and remember, "There but for the grace of God go I."

I am God's child, just like you.

CONTENTS

Chapter One

ADDICTION

There is a beast that lurks among us. It is larger than Mount Everest; deeper than the sea. It is cunning insidious and all powerful. It captures us, leaving us deaf, dumb and blind. It is our best friend and our worst enemy. It comforts us in despair, shelters us from the cold, and makes us feel warm and secure. It illicits fear, intimidation and confusion. It is narcissistic, illogical and irrational leaving its victims baffled. It is blind to whom it hurts, and how it hurts. It has no boundaries and it does not discriminate.

What is it that for a moment in time can sever our connection to God? A beast by any other name, is called addiction. When we delude ourselves, we minimize its power, making self indulgent, and anal retentive statements like, "Why don't you just stop?" "Be strong." Addiction has nothing to do with power, willpower, or constraint. By its very nature, it denotes an element of powerlessness: A dysfunctional love/hate relationship. Reference its bond, "The thought of you makes me smile. You are my only true love. I am never too far from you. And the day I am, is the day I die."

Addiction is entrenched in our society. Think about it. We live in a capitalist, self indulgent society; perpetuated by profit, greed and an incestuous desire for the extreme. More is never enough; so we go about our lives in a perpetual quest for satisfaction looking for that big win or that ultimate high. In the process, we become further alienated from ourselves and increasingly more disconnected from society. The problem is complex. Lust lives as much in our own self indulgence, as in the society in which we live. The stark reality is that, **"We live in a drug oriented, chemically dependent society."** It is not a Black thing, a white thing, an Asian thing, etc. It is not a rich thing or a poor thing. Although it is a reality that our disenfranchised communities are disproportionately affected by the insidiousness of drugs and drug related crimes, the incidence of drugs rears its ugly head on Wall Street, and in affluent communities. I am reminded of a TV commercial which shows a middle class, suburban white child skating freely through his neighborhood. The commercial goes on to state, "40% of all teenagers in the inner cities use drugs: Where do you think the other 60% of the children live?" And if that is not enough, consider a Diane Sawyer, World News Report on March 29, 2010, which spoke to the new face of heroin addiction. Reportedly, the use of heroin has skyrocketed among middle class, suburban teens. Heroin as cheap as $5.00 a bag, is being marketed under familial names such as Twilight, after the movie, to teens who start out snorting it and very quickly go on to shooting an even more powerful form of liquid heroin called Black Tar. Reportedly, the problem has escalated to the point that in suburban detoxes, there are actually more addicts than available beds.

Why do some people use drugs? Why do some people choose not to use drugs? Note, the all too familiar verbalism: "I've experienced pain and loss in life," "I've been down on my luck," "Things have not always gone my way, but I didn't use drugs." Just for one minute, let us not judge, for the purpose is clarity and enlightenment of a problem that ultimately effects all of us. So as we proceed, my only request is that we remain open to the etiology and perils of addiction. There is a saying in the world of addiction and recovery, **"There, but for the grace of God go I."** When we make judgments about others, never thinking, that this could ever happen to us, we forget, that it is only by the grace of God, that we are able to be who we are. We have acquired healthy tools: We maintain our will to make choices that are in our best interest, but, "Never say never."

Understanding why people use drugs is quite complex. We are inundated with a plethora of theories and paradigms which provide some causative factors for why people use drugs. Briefly, and as promised, very briefly, there are intra-psychic theories, which view addiction as a reflection of one's own psyche. The premise is psychological in nature and it basically looks at one's relationship to one's inner self. Attention is focused on coping skills, where the individual's ability to deal with problems is ego based; influenced by cognitive functioning, faulty thinking, or an irrational thought process.

Interpersonal theories, on the other hand, focus their attention on the individual's relationship and interactive behaviors with others. The premise is more social psychological in nature. Attention is directed to a systems approach, incorporating reference theory, peer influence and the effects of families, and groups on the individual. The assumption is that individuals are influenced by their relationship to their significant others, whereby, they internalize drug use as a norm. One's ability to maintain a sense of autonomy, preceding and following addiction, as well as recovery and or death from one's significant others are addressed in disruptive environmental theory and incomplete mourning thcory.

One's propensity to become an addict is also explained through social structural theories, which looks at how social forces influence drug taking behaviors such as race, social class, and income; specifically social adaption and learning theories are emphasized along with how our attitudes are influenced by society.

Biological theories incorporate the physiological relationship one has to drugs, including: genetic theories and predisposition, which speaks to one's susceptibility to using drugs, metabolic deficiency theory, which focuses on one's ability, or lack thereof, to break down drugs, neuro- pharmacological theory, which focuses on drug's effect on the brains' neurotransmitters, which are chemical substances which carry messages to and from the brain such as our ability to process pleasure. Remember, **addiction is a brain disease.**

We can also apply a behavioral analysis as to why some people use drugs and some do not. Predisposition factors were originally mentioned under the biological paradigm. They can also be seen through a behavioral perspective. In predisposition, susceptibility to drug use is looked at through the adolescent. This is not to say that individuals do not start using drugs until adolescence, or that they don't start until adulthood, however, statistics indicate that the average age for using drugs is fourteen, which makes adolescence a vulnerable point in the time of a child's life. The bottom line is that adolescents are more susceptible to using drugs. Adolescents go through a normal rite of passage, where in some sets, using drugs becomes a norm. It is a time they emulate adults, equating specific drug behavior with adulthood. During adolescence, individuals continue their journey as they search for some insight into who they are. Clarity or lack of clarity can be subjective; whereby often times adolescents rely on misinformation which has been acquired honestly, from inappropriate parental modeling and an inconsistent society that traditionally has glamorized certain drugs. On an individual level, we look at the person's ability to cope. Remember, it is not necessarily what happens to one in life, but how one has learned to deal with life on life terms. **"How have you learned to balance life?"** Seeking positive external supports is adaptive, however, we all don't come from a healthy environment and some of us, through our exposure, have chosen to anesthetize ourselves with chemical substances which serve as a temporary fix, but at the same time, severs our connection to self efficacy. This maladaptive response becomes learned behavior, and is internalized as an adaptive pattern. It becomes part of the addiction cycle: One has a problem, he/she seeks outside solutions in chemical substances. They are allured into a false sense of complaisance. They come down from the drugs: The problem has escalated because you did not deal with it in a timely fashion: You use again: You come down from the mind altering substance, the problem is out of control, as is one's ability to effectively resolve the problem.

An important reality in the progression of drug taking behavior is, **why you start is not why you continue.** One should reference the following account of a boy lost; yearning for a sense of self: A boy enticed by the myths, the unpredictable effects and the novelty of using drugs. How vulnerable are our young? How easily and unknowingly they get caught up in the grips of addiction never fathoming that the very drug that brings comradery and friendship brings destruction:

> I started drinking in my teens, in my house. My parents would have parties every weekend, drinking and dancing from Friday to Sunday. Everyone drank: my mother, my father, my grandmother, my grandfather, my aunts, uncles and everyone in the neighborhood. One day, I was summoned up to the roof by one of my friends. "Come up here, I want you to try something." I had heard all of the warnings about drug addiction, what would happen to you, if you became a drug addict, so I was pretty apprehensive, but hey, I was with the guys. I sat there waiting for the drug addict to surface, like I was expecting to become a drug addict right then and there. It became clear, the message I had gotten about what addiction was going to be, didn't actually happen. It was very confusing the first time around, because of my expectations, so I tried it again. A sense of wellness, a sense of joy came over me. When you smoked, your ability to laugh is multiplied. Everything seemed to have a rhythm of humor to it. Marijuana had achieved what I had been looking for. John also introduced me to LSD. He introduced me to most drugs I did in my life. I enjoyed parts of the high from LSD and parts of it, I didn't like. It kept me up for long periods of time while experiencing a lot of hallucinations. He would say, "Just remember, whatever you see, whatever you experience, you're just tripping." We'd hang together and talk about it. We managed to help each other through the trips of LSD. I went from LSD to cocaine, snorting it. It was a fantastic feeling. I felt very up; I was talkative and I felt very good, but then I didn't feel so good anymore. From cocaine, we moved into heroin because it was long lasting and it was cheap to get. I went up to this guy's

apartment and I was given a glassine envelope. I already knew how to snort, so I snorted this powder and I threw up for the next 12 hours. I felt like I had drank, but my speech wasn't slurred and I could walk. It really wasn't a very good experience, my first time out: It was pretty bad, just to throw up all day and all night. Even after the negative experience, I continued. I was assured by my friends that it would not be like that the next time, so I just continued. Eventually, I learned to enjoy it. The first drug I shot was heroin and I went from that to speed-balling. Getting high was like I was in a movie or something because one thing led to another, and before I knew it; nineteen years had passed. (Reflections of a recovering addict)

A behavioral analysis of addiction is also explained by reinforcing factors, which encourage the continued use of drugs. The expectation of pleasure, the relief of pain, stamina and endurance, are all qualities promised with certain drugs. The reinforcing effect of heroin, as shared by a recovering addict, illustrates how the experience of pleasure encourages drug use:

It was like being in your mother's womb. I felt a sense of security. Everything was alright. I didn't have anything to worry about; I was ok; I felt good. My body felt warm and I felt relaxed; I could lay back. I could do anything I wanted. Nothing bothered me. It helped me to feel like I had accomplished the American Dream without having the American Dream. It gave me everything I wanted in terms of feelings. I felt complete; I felt whole; I felt happy when I was high.

Reinforcing factors are also reflected in our advertising strategies that sometimes encourage drug use by glamorizing certain misconceptions; that using certain drugs makes one hip, cool, or more sexually appealing or "macho." One might reflect on the images of very pretty and handsome men with a drink and cigarette in their hand; socializing, having a good time.

One last behavioral analysis of drug taking behavior is enabling factors. Enabling factors facilitate one's drug use. As an enabling factor, there is no other concept more important to understanding addiction than codependency. Codependency is that complicated, interdependent relationship that exists between addicts and their significant others. The reality is that addicts could not continue their addictive patterns, if not for the enabling qualities of codependents. Codependency, in and of itself, is an addiction. Just as the addict is addicted to the drug, the codependent is addicted to the addict. The codependent's addiction is manifested by a dysfunctional, illogical thought process; a psychological projection and emotional detachment from self as they constantly become focused on the needs of others. Patterns of codependency come in many forms and can start very early in life: Case example:

> When I was young, I remember taking on the basic characteristics of codependency, that of a caretaker. My grandmother was an alcoholic, as far back as I can remember, and I used to hide her liquor bottles for her, from my grandfather. Even though I knew it was wrong and he did not want her to drink, I did it anyway. I was experiencing the characteristics of denial at a very early age.

Codependents live under the illusion that they in some way, can change the addictive patterns of the addict. They cover up and pretend the problem does not exist or that the problem is really not that bad. An example is, the "ever loving wife," making excuses for her sick, hung over, incapacitated or missing husband: "John won't be at the office today, he has the flu." The enabler makes excuses to other family members, "We won't be able to make the dinner today, Susan has another migraine," or "Be quiet, daddy is sleeping, and you know he works very hard." The codependent may also repeatedly bail the addict out of jail, pay bills and assume all of the responsibilities for the addict. The codependent may also be the wife yelling at her husband "I'm sick and tired of picking up all of your sh—t," only to be followed by compromise; doing exactly what she said she was not going to do. One should reference the following real life accounts of codependency:

> My dear sweet mother assumed the role of my caretaker. No matter what, she would take care of her 'baby boy'. When I needed money for drugs, so I wouldn't go out and get myself in trouble, she always supported me. Even though I did not tell her that I was using the money to support my habit, she knew, and she gave it to me anyway. Even as my addiction progressed, my mother was the one I could always count on to keep my addiction functioning. I remember one night, I came home exhausted after a binge of drinking and drugging, and I was attempting to sleep it off. That particular day, it had been raining all day and most of the night. I remember, my dear, sweet, enabling mother, telling my grandmother in a sympathetic voice, "He looks like he has been walking all night in the rain": All awhile never mentioning my appearance which was obviously that of an addict.

> In the words of another addict:

> Most of my addiction, I spent at one mother figure's home or another. There was a lot of praying for me, to do something about what was happening to me. For me, anything my mother had to say, I didn't want to hear, because she was trying to pull me away from the thing that made me feel like a human being. I would listen to anything she wanted to say, as long as she would help to get what I wanted to get: To feel like a human being. It started out with just a couple of dollars, just to get out and get some. I'm sure she knew, but like most good parents, she had a sense, that she would rather give me the money than have me go out and do something, hurt someone, and land up in jail. Many times I sat there and listened to her preach to me. She knew that all I was doing was letting

her blow off steam, so that she would give me the money, so I could go out there and do what I had to do.

In both accounts, the addictive nature of codependency is characterized by mother's clear minimization and denial of her son's addiction. Ultimately, codependents provide a safety net for addicts which prevents them from hitting "rock bottom." In other words, addicts never feel the consequences of their actions. Codependents enable addicts, to continue on their paths of destructive use, leaving them no reason to assume any sense of responsibility for their addiction. As the codependent's life becomes increasingly organized around the addict, as they become enmeshed, and boundaries are compromised, as self defeating behaviors incur, the codependent progressively loses all concept of his/her identity. Self worth becomes defined by everything one does for the addict, in contrast to establishing and maintaining a separate sense of self.

There is an insidious, embryonic, dualism that exists between the codependent and the addict. One cannot exist without the other. Codependency feeds addiction, and addiction thrives off of codependency. The irony of the relationship is that codependents cry, beg, and even pray, for addicts to abstain from their drug taking behaviors not realizing that the very nature of their own addiction, and their actions, not only sustains the very thing they cry out against, but ultimately leads to their own destruction.

Enabling factors are also reflected in the availability and accessibility of drugs. Simply put, the more available a drug is, the more likely one is to use. That is not to say that, just by virtue of availability and accessibility one is going to use, but that our use is facilitated by exposure. Have you ever wondered, why some people use one drug and others use another? Many times the presence of the drug entices use. Look at drinking patterns, for example. The inner cities are inundated with liquor stores, which open very early, and close very late.

Prices are competitive and there is an abundance of low end liquor in travel size and half pint containers. Suburban areas, in contrast are restricted by zoning laws, which prohibit the amount of liquor stores in any one town. Spending patterns also vary in those suburban communities which buy in bulk from wholesalers. The prevalence of other drugs is also more readily available contingent on geographical location. It stands to reason, that one is first introduced to the availability of drugs in the area in which they live. (Note: There are exceptions)

Another enabling factor which is noteworthy is the contradictions which exist in our criminal justice system. There is a positive relationship between one's perception of the legalities associated with certain drugs and the accountability for possession and use. The system tends to criminalize some drugs more harshly than others. A case in point is the 100-to-1 disparity in relation to minimum sentencing for crack and powdered cocaine where one was punished more harshly for 5 grams of crack cocaine than they were for 500 grams of powdered cocaine.

We could go on, and in more detail, about the vast theoretical paradigms that seek to understand drug taking behavior. But far be it from me, to inundate you with more theories. The reality is that **no one theory can explain why everyone uses drugs.** In addition, the causative factors are as unique as any one individual. Theories, therefore, should not be taken for an all inclusive explanation. They are a reference point that speaks to the infinite possibilities of why one uses drugs. Addicts are also complex. We do them a disservice, if we try to understand them from one perspective. Any one individual is a culmination of a historical self, an economic self, a religious and political self, and a physiological and psychological self. The bottom line is that, in order to understand addiction, one has to assess each person as an individual. One can't fit people into nice little theoretical boxes. This being said, the impending focus will be less theory orientated, and more practical in-terms of identifying those variables which are inextricably tied to addiction.

Chapter Two

SELF ESTEEM

Don't be fooled by me. Don't be fooled by the face I wear.

For I wear a mask. I wear a thousand mask, mask that I am afraid to take off, and none of them is me, but don't be fooled, for God's sake don't be fooled.

I give you the impression that I'm secure, that all is sunny and unruffled with me, within as well as without.

That confidence is my name and coolness is my game, and that I need no one.

But don't believe me. My surface is my mask.

Beneath dwells the real me in confusion, in fear, in aloneness.

But I hide this. I don't want anyone to know it.

I panic at the thought of my weakness and fear being exposed.

That's why I frantically create a mask to hide behind, to shield me from the glance that knows.

But such a glance is precisely my salvation-that is, if it is followed by acceptance, by love.

It's the only thing that can liberate me of what I can't assure myself-that I'm really worth something.

But I'm afraid to tell you this; I'm afraid that your glance will not be followed by acceptance and love.

I'm afraid you'll laugh, and that laugh will kill me.

I idly chatter to you in the suave tones of surface talk.

I tell you everything that's really nothing, and nothing of what's everything or what is crying within me.

Please listen carefully and try to hear what I'm not saying, what I would like to be able to say.

I'd really like to be genuine and spontaneous, and me, but you've got to help me.

You alone can release me from my shadow world of panic and uncertainty, from my lonely prison.

It will not be easy for you.

A long conviction of worthlessness builds strong walls.

I am irrational-I fight against the very thing that I cry out for.

But I am told that love is stronger than strong walls.

Please try to beat down those strong walls with firm hands, but with gentle hands-for I am very sensitive.

Who am I, you may wonder.

I am someone you 'know' very well, I am every man you meet and I am every woman you meet. (Author Unknown)

What fragile beings we are. What lengths we go through to protect ourselves. We hide behind half grins, and superficial smiles- acting as if. How much energy is exhausted in playing the game? We spew common phrases, "Oh, I'm al----right," "I'm fine." In the world of addiction and recovery, fine is an acronym for "f—cked up," insecure, neurotic and emotional, so how are we really? We wear mask while deluded in the illusion that "I'm Ok"; "You're Ok." For some, we are fragile, scared children, full of self doubt and fearful of failure while playing grown-up in an adult world. How important is our self esteem and what is its' relationship to addiction?

"The most important factor effecting behavior is the self concept. The self is the star of every performance, the central figure in every act."

There is no concept more important to understanding addiction than self esteem. **Addiction is an ego disease.** Although self esteem is a common component linking addicts together, every addict is truly unique. They are separated by their relationship to their drug of choice, and more importantly, they are separated by their relationship to self. **Self esteem and addiction are inextricably related.** They cannot be separated. To grasp the complexities of addiction one must be in tuned to the symbiotic bond between addiction and self esteem. Addiction starts with the individual. **You are your addiction, and your addiction is you.**

The need for human approval becomes the chief determinant of who we are, and who we become. Self esteem is learned; we are not born to feel bad about ourselves. As infants, we learn to differentiate between self and others. Those others are paramount in shaping our self concept. Self image is formed through reflective appraisals and social comparisons: "You'll never amount to anything," "You're a loser," "You're stupid," "You're just like your father," "You're too fat, too dark," "You've ruined my life, I could have been..." "You're better off dead." All of these statements have a profound effect on individuals. One addict states: "I felt different than everyone else, I wanted to protect my image, to be accepted and recognized."

How we perceive ourselves is first interpreted by our perception of how others perceive us. Addicts often assume other images from their perception of whom or what is respected in society. Reference Cooley's, "looking glass self", or Mead's, "taking the role of the other." Consistent ridicule and incriminations foster feelings of worthlessness, helplessness, and hopelessness, while all the while, we continually view our world with pessimism. It is really tough to understand our identities when we continually receive messages from parents, relatives, friends, teachers, and mainstream America about who we are in contrast to who we should be. These messages penetrate our soul. We hear and we listen, internalizing these messages as expectations which become self fulfilling prophecies. Self esteem must be cultivated and nurtured from the ground up. "It is indeed a slippery slope," and incredibly difficult to gain. Positive self esteem is like a stair case. You start at the bottom; accomplishments and positive endeavors help to raise you to a higher step. Without the fundamentals and support at an early age, one cannot climb the staircase. An addict substantiates this in the following statement: "I started off with low self esteem. If it wasn't for all of those years of crap in my life, I wouldn't have such low self esteem, such low expectations. I would always feel like I'm not going anywhere, anyway."

Self esteem is a combination of self confidence and self respect. It is the idea that one is competent and able to cope with life challenges;

that one is worthy of happiness. Self esteem is personal efficacy, the feeling of empowerment that one can be all that one wants to be; it is a sense of personal self worth that one is in fact deserving of all that is good. I am reminded of the inspiration of Jessie Jackson: "If your mind can conceive it, and your heart can believe it, you can be anything you want to be."

For some individuals, however, the seed of poor self esteem is planted early in their personal lives. Unresolved feelings, self doubt, and incrimination, create a void, an emptiness; which makes it difficult for them to accept themselves. **Incapable of overcoming challenges, addicts seek refuge in their addictions.** Individual thinking becomes distorted. Addicts are not even comfortable with their own personal strengths. Dignity, value and the understanding that one is a unique human being is shadowed by an ominous past. And the only solace is in getting high. In the words of another addict:

> I felt a sense of security, everything was alright. I didn't have anything to worry about; I felt good. My body felt warm; my mind felt relaxed. I could do anything I wanted. I felt complete and I felt whole; I felt happy when I was high. It was only when I wasn't high that I felt uncomfortable.

Addiction is not a weakness or a moral deficiency. The truth for many addicts is that they have become displeased with where and who they are. It becomes a viable alternative for an individual to turn to a substance, to drown the pain, in contrast to living with self.

> Addiction is an attachment to something or someone outside of yourself that you feel you need to provide a sense of inner satisfaction or relief. The preoccupation with the reality of one's existence is filled with the drug. It may also substitute a temporary feeling of control of power for a more lasting sense of inner confidence and strength. (www.open-mind.org)

Reflect on the illusion of strength and power the addict achieves when using cocaine or other stimulant drugs, or the splendorous day dreams with heroin, or the dulling of the sharp edges of reality with alcohol which is described in the user's own words:

> The warm feeling that I get when I first started doing it, that warm feeling in my stomach. I felt euphoria. It took away the loneliness. I got a sense of power, a sense I could do things, confidence, I could take on the world.

To deal with the emotion of low self esteem addicts numb themselves by minimizing pain and escaping to a world which allows a temporary fix from problems and suffering as an addict describes in the following: "I had found God: I had found Nirvana. I didn't need anything else but this. As long as I had this, I was happy. The world could die, fall apart. Family: I didn't care about anything as long as I was high."

If self esteem is a way of thinking, feeling and acting that implies that one respects one's self, addicts are caught up in the vicious cycle of addiction that compromises their self concept. At this stage in their addiction, "They are living to use and using to live." Driven by addiction, they are not concerned with how they look or how others perceive them. **In this moment of space and time, the driving force in their lives is self preservation.** Preoccupation is with sustaining their addiction in order to avoid any uncomfortability, be it from withdrawal or negative self incrimination.

Chapter Three

POWERLESSNESS

I walk down the street; there is a deep hole in the sidewalk;

I fall in.

I am lost; I am hopeless: It isn't my fault;

it takes forever to find a way out.

I walk down the same street; there is a deep hole in the sidewalk;

I pretend I don't see it.

I fall in again.

I can't believe I am in the same place, but it isn't my fault:

It still takes a long time to get out.

I walk down the same street; there is a deep hole in the sidewalk;

I see it is there:

I still fall in; it's a habit (Portia Nelson)

(Reprinted with the permission of Atria Books, Division of Simon & Schuster, Inc, from "There's a Whole In My Sidewalk: The Romance of Self Discovery" by Portia Nelson. Copyright @1993 by Portia Nelson. All rights reserved.)

One is reminded of the uniqueness of each individual, and as such, the uniqueness of each addiction. Not negating this reality, there is a thread of consistency which runs through all addictions. How many times have we asked addicts to stop using drugs by referencing the pain they are inflicting on themselves and their love ones. How can some individuals drink themselves into oblivion, smoke even though they know it is unhealthy, shop until they are broke, gamble through their life savings, engage in promiscuous relationships with multiple partners, and break the trust and bond between themselves, their spouses and children. The answer is really quite simple. **Addicts can't stop: They are powerless over their addiction.** It is the compulsive nature of addiction that makes the addict powerless. Powerlessness denotes a lack of control over one's life. It is a state of mind that can be both physical and mental which allows the drug or the behavior to be the focal point in the addict's life. ***The obsession to gratify the addiction can absolutely cripple addicts as they become consumed with their drug.***

Because of the progressive nature of addiction and the sense of powerlessness, the addiction takes over one's daily life. Addicts develop habits and rituals which feed the insatiable desire to experience the pleasures of their addiction. The addiction is exacerbated by a sense of powerlessness, engaging in a drug almost against their will. Reference the following account:

"It's like climbing a tree, knowing you are afraid of heights, but you do it anyway. You take one step further and you go out on the

branch and you are stuck out there: You can't get down. Oh God, if the branch breaks, I'm going to die." Now a logical person would see imminent danger and retreat. The addict, however, is driven by a sense of powerlessness. Addiction, that sense of powerlessness knows no logic. Logically, one is able to retreat, but addicts are compelled to pursue that activity. The sense of powerlessness is really brought home in the following account:

> I was struggling with myself: Why do I keep yearning for it? Why do I want to go back to it? Before I knew it, I was sitting somewhere: I had bought the drug. I was sitting in a shooting gallery, tears rolling down my eyes, because I felt so powerless. Why couldn't I stop myself? Why couldn't I control myself? And then that feeling came back: the feeling of security, the feeling of warmth, that feeling that I needed to survive. I felt like I could not be without the drug in my system. I am 7 ½ months pregnant, I don't want my baby to be on drugs. I cried, I walked home after copping, and I kept crying.

Have you ever wanted to do something so bad, and you just couldn't. Each time you tried, you failed. Remember that sense of powerlessness you felt. Maybe, it was trying to lose weight or save money. Or maybe going up for that promotion that was in your pocket, only to be beat out by someone who was less qualified. As bad as you felt, that sense of powerlessness that consumed you is the same feeling that cripples the addict. Knowing that on one level he/she doesn't want the drug, but somehow the need to indulge is overpowering.

The insidious side of powerlessness is that often times, one does not even know when he/she becomes powerless. One starts off just having a good time, then finds more and more legitimate reasons to use: Promotions, celebrations, get-togethers, and because of the progressive nature of the disease of addiction, before one knows it, one has crossed the line as reflected in the following: "Somewhere down the line, I lost all touch and points of reality. I never knew when I crossed the line. People would tell me something is wrong, something is different: All I knew was that I had to use." Another addict relates:

> I got high in all different places with all different people. I tried moderation, no such thing. I tried stashing, that didn't work. I'd carry ups when doing downs and downs when doing ups. I tried to be a dealer and I became my own best customer. I tried going to bars and drinking orange juice, that would work in that bar, then I would go down the street to another bar and get drunk. I went to school to become a substance abuse counselor. I achieved a 4.0 average and my CAC educational hours, so I went out to get high to celebrate, not to mention that I learned new techniques and strategies to cure myself.

A third addict relates: "Oh my God! Am I caught up in this cycle? How will I get off? Will I be able to get off? That's when it really set in. I had crossed the line."

Many of us believe that the addict continues to get high, despite our pleas because he or she just doesn't want to stop, or one doesn't love us enough to stop. At this point in the addiction, love and desire have nothing to do with the ability to stop using drugs. **For some addicts, every night they get high is followed by a morning and a commitment to stop using the drug.** Powerlessness means not being in control of that intent as the following shows: "I wanted to stop getting high, but I couldn't, I didn't know how, I felt like I had lost control."

Initially, it was stated, that why we start using the drug is not why we continue. The following validates that notion:

> It was a fun thing to do, a recreational habit. Then it's, I want to get high, I need to get high. There was a sense of powerless-ness, the consuming nature of addiction. From that point the

drug became me and I became the drug. I could feel it in my brain, I could feel it in my mouth, I could feel it in my entire body, but it didn't last, and I was left with that feeling that I needed more. And then there is a point where you get high even though you don't want to. Why am I doing this? I know this doesn't feel good anymore. You are sitting there getting high by yourself. Why are you doing this, you feel miserable. You ain't got no money and you ain't got no food in the house; now what are you going to do?

The sense of powerlessness can also be complicated by the physical nature of addiction. The physiological impact, for example, of cocaine on the brain, creates a physical urgency of powerlessness. In simple terms, **"It's like Lay's Potato Chips, you can't eat just one."** So you find yourself engaging in uncontrollable behavior. With crack, for example, it is often referred to as "going on a mission." The mission is the repetitive behavior where one gets high, comes down, gets high, 24/7, for days on end, until one is physiologically and emotionally drained: One crashes, sleeps for 24-48 hours, wakes up, eats, and resumes one's mission. That pursuit, described in the following, reflects the powerlessness of the disease: "Why am I doing this again? I know I don't like the feeling. There is more time spent on looking for drugs, looking for money, trying to find out where it is, the pursuit of more, more, more."

Powerlessness is the inability to stop using a substance. **Addiction and powerlessness are inextricably related.** The obsessive compulsive nature leaves the addict with an uncontrollable drive to secure the drug. So the addict chases a particular feeling. The sad reality is that those desires, the satiation of those feelings, are only produced in the minds' of each victim: illusions of control, illusions of security.

Chapter Four

DENIAL

Early on in my process of addiction I had convinced myself that it was normal to get up in the morning and go to the refrigerator and down a 40 oz beer for breakfast with a joint I left in the ashtray the night before. There was nothing wrong with getting a little high before first period when I was in the 10th grade. There was nothing wrong with leaving the math class in third period to meet up with a few friends in the boy's bathroom, one of which had went to the store to bring back a quart of beer for us to share with lose joints that we purchased on the way to school. There was absolutely nothing wrong with this behavior, it was normal. It was normal to break into my neighbor's apartment and steal her jewelry while she was on vacation in Jamaica; besides the lock on the door was broken, so it wasn't like I was breaking in. This type of behavior was acceptable. As my addiction progressed, so did my level of denial. This addiction of mine had me thinking that I was getting high when all of the time, I was getting low. Of course the reality of it was that I was still young and in the early stage of my addiction, the alcohol had not begun to take its toll. As time and the addiction moved on, the denial told me that it was ok to wake up throwing up my guts the next morning after drinking vodka the night before. Denial led me to believe that if the vodka didn't agree with me, then I should seek a different type of alcohol that would not produce the same reaction. Perhaps gin or rum might do the trick and if that didn't work, keep trying until I found the right potion. My addiction had me believing that no matter what, it was ok to continue the path of slow destruction; that I was following everybody that I associated with that did what I did-get high. Denial had me believing that it was ok to get behind the wheel of an automobile while intoxicated. I was still very much in control. Besides, my first accident wasn't my fault. The parked car that I hit was sitting too far from the curb. Because I was in denial, this became a normal thing for me. As a matter of fact, I began drinking and driving at the same time; first beers and then hard liquor. There is a statistic that says the normal alcoholic probably drives drunk at least one hundred times before they receive their first DWI: Please, I had that beat at least by a hundred. As soon as I got my car, my first stop was to the store to get a beer. My denial became so strong, that when the police finally did catch me driving while intoxicated, I believed that they couldn't smell the liquor on my breath and actually questioned the results of the breathalyzer. The denial was so strong that it had me believing, I did not have a problem. So what, I was shot at and missed and "shitted" on and hit. I did not consider myself with the problem. I was not homeless living in a card board box. I didn't realize, that if it wasn't for my mother, I would be homeless and might need some card board to keep me warm at night. I had a mental block named denial that told me, I was not an addict. I could stop getting high, if I wanted to. It didn't matter that alcoholism was prevalent in my family: Grandmother, grandfather, father, mother, aunts, and uncles: Everybody drank, therefore, this behavior was acceptable.

DENIAL, Don't Even Know I Am Lying. Denial is an automatic and unconscious defense mechanism that we all use to protect self, thoughts, and feelings from the reality of our own existence. If we are human, we are in denial about something; some aspect of ourselves, our behavior, our health, our family, or our relationships. Most of us strive for everything in our lives to be comfortable and fine. When we are threatened by uncomfortable truths, denial is the cloud that shields us, the wall that protects us, allowing selective awareness and minimizing all that is painful. Denial is a symptom of addiction. It allows the addiction to thrive, to stay alive. It is neither deliberate nor willful. It is a psychological process by which addicts protect themselves with tremendous vigor by blocking out knowledge of any and all things that threaten their existence. Once an individual enters the process of addiction, it is very difficult to elude the grips of denial as the following statement of an addict shows: "I could tell myself anything and believe it. Yeah: I'm okay man. Don't worry about it: I can deal with it. You can psych yourself up to believe anything: Everything is in the head." Denial is a defense that distorts reality. It stops addicts from feeling the pain and the sharp realities of truth about things that they do not want to face. It blinds addicts to the cause of their dependence on drugs. It allows them to pretend that their using is not devastating even when it is. Denial is a partial truth about a small part of reality; as if it were all true. The individual, for example who has not used drugs in the last few hours might assert, "I haven't been using," conveniently leaving out the reality that, a few hours ago, they had in fact, gotten high.

The destructive consequences of addiction may be apparent to everyone, with the exception of the addict, despite the fact that there is glaring evidence to the contrary. Logic and rationality does not make a difference. In the words of an addict: "I had to stay away from them. I didn't want them to know, even though they knew anyway."Addicts believe their own denial to avoid the painful reality that addiction has control over their lives, that their lives are spiraling out of control. They may deny help because they don't want to feel helpless or powerless. Generally, people don't want to feel powerless, helpless, and out of control. Addicts may use denial to mask the consequences of their actions, which allows them to continue to live without making changes. **Denial thrives, and addiction lives, by any means necessary. It lives at the heart of addiction.** Denial can be a disease, in and of itself, in that, by its very nature, it is progressive.

If left untreated, in its maladaptive form, it can be fatal. Denial is insidious, and it is a necessary evil of addiction. It takes on many forms, and addicts use all of them to perpetuate and sustain their addictions.

For addicts, simple denial exists in the very assertion that they are not an addict: "You know you have a problem," "No I don't." Reference the account of the addict in the opening passage. Denial permeates his addiction as it becomes increasingly more progressive. Denial is further evidenced through the following behavior: Rationalization is used as addicts give excuses for their behavior, "Everyone I associate with does what I do." They take no responsibility for their part in using drugs. The following reference is from another addict:

> The more you get high, the more you drink, so one went hand in hand with the other. So you're really an alcoholic and a drug addict, but you can't see the alcoholism because you are too busy becoming a drug addict. And then you start to rationalize: Yeah, well I did drink a fifth of Remy Martin, but I didn't get drunk, so I'm not an alcoholic. Your mind is too weird because it rationalizes everything bad that you do.

Justification helps addicts validate their behavior, "I needed money for marijuana and beer, and I didn't have any." Blaming projects the responsibility for one's behavior on to someone else, "The first accident wasn't my fault. The parked car that I hit was too far from the curb." Minimization takes the sting out of the problem to some degree, "There's nothing wrong with getting a little high before first period." Minimization is further demonstrated from this reference: "All of the other drugs, they weren't so bad: I had been in control. With crack, I lost it. It made me run more in terms of having to get the drug." Please note, that there is a reality in the notion that the pursuit of crack is relentless; however, the idea that he was in control of all of the other drugs clearly reaffirms his denial and minimizes his addiction. By its very nature, addiction denotes a lack of control. Intellectualization allows the addict to disassociate from emotional realities, by hiding behind proposed facts: "The vodka didn't agree with me, I should try another type of alcohol," "I actually questioned the results of the breathalyzer," "Alcoholism was prevalent in my family: Grandmother, grandfather, father, mother, aunts, and uncles: Everybody drank." Consider an example of intellectualization from another addict: "I have always been a strong person underneath all of that. Take cigarettes, for instance. I could smoke for five years, two packs a day, just smoke, smoke, smoke and just one day, I wouldn't smoke anymore. I don't know, my body has just been able to tell me when I had enough." In this account, the denial is conveniently selective. He references his strength and his physiological tolerance, but one must not lose site of the reality that for many addicts, **the concept of "enough" is diametrically opposed to addiction.**

Other commonly used defenses that fall under denial are: bargaining, when the addict attempts to manipulate their own use by "cutting deals" with significant others, "If you stop, I will stop;" passivity is when the addict plays the victim, "I can't stop, this thing is bigger than me," and of course the ultimate denial, "I don't have a problem," and "I can stop getting high when I want to."

Each of these defenses represents subtypes of denial that are an emotional rejection of the truth. Denial distorts the addict's perception of reality and makes it impossible to accurately see the severity of his/her addiction. Entwined in addiction, denial becomes automatic and hand in hand, the disease of addiction and the disease of denial become increasingly pervasive. Ultimately, addicts are unable to distinguish between fantasy and reality. In other words, **they don't even know they are lying.**

Chapter Five

ANGER

Anger is generally defined as a strong feeling of hostility. It is a state of emotional excitement induced by intense displeasure as a result of real or imagined threat, insult, put down, frustration or injustice to yourself or to others who are important to you. (Carlson, MD. 1981). In the words of Benjamin Franklin, "Anger is never without reason but seldom a good one."

Anger is a complex concept to clarify: What is it, what does it feel like? It is certainly a normal human emotion, experienced by all, sometimes justifiable, sometimes irrational. It is a feeling that needs to be expressed and quite frankly, it is okay to express it within reason. How we express it plays a vital role in our well being. The well adjusted individual has developed effective strategies to process, to place in perspective and to let go of anger. They have learned to separate themselves from the person effecting them, and they realize that to get angry at someone else empowers them and compromises self. For the addict, however, anger is an underlying source for addiction in that drugs have become a maladaptive coping mechanism which serves to mask real problems. **For the addict, there is an intricate web that is tangled between anger and addiction.** Addicts don't always connect their anger to drugs, but in some manner, every time they pick them up, there is some form of anger that accompanies usage whether it is internalized or externalized. Ultimately, the pursuit of soothing pain generated by the anger becomes the driving force for the addict to use.

For the addict, anger is like a drug and one can develop an anger habit. **Strong anger has a speedball effect.** The anger outburst, like thunder and lightning, is comparable to the cocaine rush that makes you feel powerful; the anger subsides, and one feels a sense of relief like the very relaxed feeling produced by heroin. **Anger, therefore, is a God given feeling that provides a medium to feeling alive in the face and agony of nothingness and deadness.** When addicts become angry, they become both mentally and physically stimulated. Consider the release of adrenaline which elevates one's heart rate and blood pressure: Let go of the anger, fill in the blanks, rational suicide. How is suicide rational? It is the inevitable outcome culminating in perpetual peace. So one is consumed with anger and rage, one anesthetizes those feelings with drugs, and one's faulty thinking enables suicide. There is a method to the madness. Anger does not kill, but the actions we take as humans do.

Anger is one of the most powerful of human emotions. Some addicts use it as a natural defense to ward of any attack or threat to their well being. Anger is not the problem: It is the mismanagement of angry feelings, which for some is the fuel that has propelled them into despair. For the addict, anger can come from many different directions. It can be displeasure for what we regard as a wrong towards us, such as sexual abuse, violence, abandonment, as well as directed at family siblings, peers and even strangers who become victims of our displaced wrath as stated by a drug abuser: "All my life, I did things to make other people angry. I wanted to get back at them because they made me so angry. You made me live in this house of hell." For the addict, anger can be a hostile feeling, a ticking time bomb which becomes prevalent in their lives, and as they become entangled in the dangerous cycle of anger, it can potentially consume their lives. The loss of control over one's life becomes so overwhelming that they become angry with not only the world around them but even themselves.

For the addict, anger represents the illusion of control. They are deceived in the prospect of covering the pain, but the reality of un-control further exacerbates the problem and anger more frequently becomes one of the main defense mechanisms to avoid dealing with the reality of the situation. As the anger increases, it builds pressure contributing to explosive and destructive behavior. Consequently, it materializes into violent acts. More times than not, however, the anger is drawn inward leading to addictive, self defeating behavior. Anger and addiction can lead to a lonely and dark place within the emotional realm of the addict. In the words of an addict, "I can't keep a job, no one wants to hire an alcoholic, I can't give up my drinking by myself, I have no control, I feel like a failure." The addiction, therefore, neutralizes the anger to the point where addicts are not able to identify it. The anger festers and spills over to their surroundings and to everyone within their peripheral environment until they totally surrender to the anger and become selfless, volatile beings. The anger clouds their visibility to see clearly the toxic reality, otherwise known as their life.

Ironically, addicts also are angered when others attempt to distract them from their primary focus of getting high. That is all of the people who try to prevent them from using. In this regard, addicts can be narcissistic; getting high for them is by any means necessary. They are not in tuned to the consequences of their addiction on their significant others, who constantly chastise them about their drug use. Although the intent by others may be constructive, by the very nature of the insanity of the situation, often words can be destructive. Focusing on the addict's frailties and unmanageability, sometimes encourages addicts to look at themselves. In that brief moment, there may be clarity and what they see they may not like, and the reality of their situation, coupled with the constant criticism and agitation of others, angers them. Consequently, as in response to everything in their lives, they get high. In some regard the anger is displaced. The addicts' use is not only about those that stand in the way of them and their drug, but it is really a reflection of how angry they are at themselves. Now they are angry at others for chastising them, they are angry because others get in the way of themselves and their drug, and they are angry at themselves because they are caught up in a vicious maze with no apparent way out as reflected in the following:

> Every time someone tries to lecture me about the dangers of drugs, it pisses me off, and my response instantly is to go get high. Over and over again, why don't you stop? I reach my boiling point, and tell them to mind their own business, or I begin to point out their problems or addictions, so I can take the focus of off me. It's my choice and I understand the consequences. I am grown and if I choose to use, it is my right to do so. There are times I feel like I am being violated: I am tired of being treated like a second class citizen.

Addicts can also be angry because of the lack of funds and resources for sustaining their high. They have exhausted family, friends and all visible means of support. We know all of those people they irrationally feel are violating them, and now they are just angry. But addicts are very resourceful; remember, by any means necessary, and that reality and the uncomfortability of withdrawal is not an option. So, out of anger and desperation, come ingenious ideas and not too long after, the addict is getting high.

Chapter Six

DEPRESSION

The depression is so real: It's like a little person in your head talking to you. You get high to get away from him and now he is right back in your ear. Before he was whispering to you, and you can kinda shake him off. Now he is screaming in your ear; I mean he is screaming, loud, so loud in fact, it makes you talk back to him. Sometimes I feel like I can just cut him out: It would make me feel better, just get him right out of my ear; just flush him out and down the toilet. When I get high, he shuts up for a minute and I don't have to feel anything. But then he comes back. Have you ever seen an addict mumbling to themselves? They're talking to that little man in their head, because he is screaming in their ear.

Does drug addiction spawn depression or does depression increase the likelihood of drug abuse? The chicken and egg debate continues to be an ongoing topic of discussion. What we do know is that there is a close connection between the two, and in fact, it is quite difficult to tell where one starts and the other begins. When addiction and depression occur together, they are called co-morbid or co-occurring disorders.

It is quite normal to feel depressed after experiencing some disappointment, frustration, setback, or even traumatic events. Broken relationships, job loss, eviction, and financial hardships are common realities we all face. Once again, our ability to cope, to process these events are specific to the coping mechanisms and strategies we have learned throughout our lives. Depression, however, is a very serious illness, and when left untreated, it can be a debilitating disease which disrupts our thinking process as well as our overall body functioning. Depressed people spend more time alone, withdraw from social contacts, and become more and more unmotivated when it comes to seeking out healthy and supportive relationships.

The promise of relief can be very alluring, leading some of us to self medicate with drugs which provide temporary relief from feelings of sadness and guilt as exemplified by an addict in the following:

> I was really feeling so bad about everything that happened. I was looking for a way to punish myself, especially when I felt guilty. To take away that feeling, I felt like I had to use more and more to anesthetize those feelings. I was feeling really guilty. I would do anything to live a normal life.

The depression is only made worse by the drugs and it becomes a vicious cycle. Continued use leads to addiction, and depending upon the drug, the frequency of use and the length of drug dependence, there are fundamental changes which occur in the brain which compromises one's ability to function. Addicts face a wide range of feelings, moods and emotions. Their inability to experience pleasure predicated on feelings of sadness and hopelessness, becomes overwhelming and consumes their lives. In the process of addiction, addicts develop an intimate relationship with depression. Because they have not developed the ability to live life on life terms, drugs represent a promise of comfort and relief. Ironically, however, addicts are depressed when they are high and when they are sober. The depression is aggravated by their preoccupation with obtaining their next high. Even if addicts have the financial means to obtain their drug, the compulsiveness of the disease dominates their life: Where to go, who to see, will I get the most for what I have? The mind races as addicts are driven by their compulsion to use. In the cycle of addiction, one's ability to think logically and rationally is compromised. Although one originally sought out the drug for relief from depressive thoughts, using leads one right back to depression as an addict attest to in the following statement: "Why did I do this again? What was I thinking? I should have gone somewhere else. I'm not going to do this again. What is wrong with me? Why can't I stop? Oh God, please no more: Just let me die." When addicts come face to face with the realization of the destruction they have caused in their lives, they become depressed. The depression stirs up feelings of hopelessness and loss of control enticing the addict to use again to escape the painful emotions as reflected in the following by another user: "I was depressed after coming down from the high. I felt worthless and disappointed in myself. I would cry all of the time."

Depression shows its ugly face time and time again. Even when the addict is high, with the "accuracy of a Timex Watch," right at the time that the high starts to descend, the feelings of depression kick up as illustrated in the following account: "The immediate feeling of euphoria is replaced as soon as the drug wears off causing a deeper depression with fatigue, guilt and anxiety."

One must also consider the physiological component that connects depression and addiction; both share the same regions of the brain. Remember, drugs work in relation to specific chemicals in the brain called neurotransmitters. Each neurotransmitter maintains a particular bodily task ensuring a state of equilibrium. The neurotransmitter serotonin, for example, not only effects sensory perception, sleep, body temperature, but mood. There are certain drugs like ecstasy, for example, which effect serotonin. When you use ecstasy, you increase the production of serotonin. Depending on how much you take, frequency, and your unique biochemistry; If you substantially deplete serotonin, when your body needs it to keep you balanced emotionally, you do not have enough of it to stabilize your mood. It is a reality that individuals who abuse ecstasy often suffer from depression. In addition, one must consider how certain drugs place one in a depressed state. Drugs are classified by how they affect the central nervous system. Depressant drugs, depress the nervous system. Alcohol, for example, is a depressant. Although many people drink because they are depressed, with the expectation of feeling better, the initial surge of exuberation is a pseudo-stimulation, meaning that it is temporary, an initial stage of the alcohol state of consciousness. Ultimately, one will experience the depressant qualities of alcohol, which when taken in excess, can lead to sleeping, or a decline in REM sleeping, a constant state of depression and even death. Marijuana, the drug that many know and love, is not categorized as a depressant, but it has depressant like effects; consequently, it can lead to depression. Heroin, although not in the same category as marijuana also has depressant like effects. Cocaine, crack cocaine, amphetamines, methamphetamines are stimulants; they speed up the central nervous system. When you first use them, you experience a rush, "bam," sometimes even an orgasm, specifically, in the case of crack. The descent, however, is a crash causing depression. According to one addict:

> The depression won't set in until you start to come down, because it does something to you. Physically it makes you feel bad, really bad. The depression set in, because I was just getting high too much. The coke made me so high, but then you would come down, so low. If it wasn't for all of those years of crap in your life.

Another addict says:

> I started to feel depressed…now I really felt low: I did something to get high, and now I am not high. It was like offering a piece of candy to a kid, and then taking it away from them. I got that glorious sensation and then it's gone and in its place,

> I had this extreme sense of depression, so then I would do more.

And still another addict relates:

> It wasn't that float me up kinda high. It was really an intense kinda high. I never thought this was true. Crack made me "come," it really does. You really have an orgasm right away. And that's what catches you, that orgasm. And the funny thing about it was, I couldn't have sex.

Benzodiazepine drugs, which are the psychotropic medications prescribed by psychiatrist for mood and anxiety disorders, can also cause depression as a side effect. The availability of these drugs by street pharmacist and the resourceful manner in which addicts use and abuse these drugs can cause depression and potential fatalities when they combine the drug with other illicit drugs, thereby causing a synergistic or potentiating effect. The faster the addict comes down from their high, the stronger the depression. The compulsive thought tells the addict that he/she must get back to that state that he/she was in before the descent. The irony is that the addict will never experience the same intensity of the drug twice. Every high is relatively different because our thought process fluctuates; our mindset and emotional stability varies effecting the nature of the "high," and tolerance increases which is the body's ability to become more effective at metabolizing (breaking down) the drug.

Depression takes the addict for another ride. The depression becomes chronic, the disease of addiction becomes progressive and they are both at war debilitating the addict into a further state of depression. Of course, within the vicious, self defeating reaction of the addict, he/she responds to all that is insanity with more insanity; they get "high," and the insanity continues.

Chapter Seven

ISOLATION

Wet, dark, alone, naked in a closet

Walking by a liquor store and asking, "just a bag full"

Rejected, turning away, a return to the shadows

Isolation and addiction, on the backs of clouds dreaming self into the sky never feeling more connected a million miles away.

The ride to buy is mission impossible providing no more thought than that required for selecting a choice of penny candy.

Isolation from reality becomes a collection of disassociated associates

Faces without names, I'm Ok, you're not

Fuel for mass isolation

The good guys are the enemy and your worst enemy, your best friend

A top secret mission is not looking to conspicuous

Isolation is the end result of disassociation from self

A departure from the many self woven, self defeating behaviors driven by an attitude

Isolation, a retreat exchanged for the illusion of being in control

The delusion of the great magnificent Oz billowing great and profound emptiness bearing little to no concern for those whom may be affected. (Anonymous recovering addict)

What is isolation? Is it the state of being alone, seclusion, solitude, separation? You have heard that all too familiar saying, by John Donne, "No man is an island." Human beings are social animals; they are not meant to be alone. It all comes down to, why am I alone? I think all of us require some quiet time to regroup, refocus and process life on life's terms, but what about others who are sad and lonely creatures, who isolate because they are avoiding something?

If it is difficult for you to relate, **think of how easy it is for a "normal" person to isolate.** Sometimes a victim of circumstance, a child with an empty smile may feel very much alone; alienated from preoccupied and/or addicted parents, whose idea of good parenting skills is a nanny, material toys, and "legitimate" broken promises. The child who is lost in a family feeling resentful and disconnected because their parents are unable to provide them with material comfort, which sometimes brings on a false sense of security. There are children at school who are isolated because of some perceived difference between themselves and their peers; this isolation encouraged with our advancing technological society where we can enter a virtual world and assume whole new identities. The elderly who are shunned by a society that demonizes aging and treats them like lepers by abusing and abandoning them. Their best friend becomes a drink or a pill which comforts them and soothes the sharp edges of their "menial existence."

How sad we are: How easy it is to feel isolated. From the root of isolation comes loneliness that we camouflage with business, activities, participation, relationships, places and things. Most of us don't know how we become isolated, especially if we are coming from what is assumed to be a so called good home, where everything appears to be fine. Most of us are caught up in addictive patterns and cycles that are repetitive which can be negative or positive, but definitely negative when we no longer have a choice but to do them impulsively. Perhaps you know someone, whose only contact with others involves constant rampages about what they have bought, how much it cost, or where they are going now? Sound familiar? This denotes **a false ego, from a lonely, isolated individual.** We are really unhappy, and we seek to find answers in things. We may have will power in some things and be very successful, but all of the bravado is a mask. Underneath lays a very lonely individual.

The use of drugs can start out casually or socially but the increased social usage can turn into abuse which can progress into dependence. Isolation precedes and follows addiction as seen in the following: "I would get what I needed to get high, take everything in the house, because I knew once I went in, I would lock the door: I wasn't coming back out."

Isolation is an unconscious defense mechanism that mainly occurs when the individual's involvement with the substance becomes an obsession. The disease is progressive and social isolation is progressive. **Addiction leads to isolation and the deterioration of normal, healthy relationships.** Addicts become seriously isolated, emotionally and physically from family and friends and nearly everyone else. They feel that they have to stay away from people because they don't want them to know, even though they know.

They begin to make themselves scarce. A family member relates:

> I began to see and hear less and less from her. Slowly she withdrew from me. Having no idea of what was going on, I began to try to contact her with no response. I was distraught, thinking I had done something to make her mad at me. Finally, I made contact with her, only to have her admit that she was using again. She had isolated herself from me entirely. I try often to get her to do things with me, but my attempts have been unsuccessful. It is hard as an outsider to have someone close isolate themselves from you. I know and understand that this is part of her addiction, but it is so hard to deal with. She needs help, and I can't do anything to help her. I can only hope that she will seek the help she needs.

Addicts may feel embarrassed, misunderstood and rejected, or their isolation may be a way to hide the addiction, or just a tactic to be alone to maintain the addiction. They do not believe that others would want to be around them. Remember, **one can be in a room full of people and feel very much alone.** Reference the following:

> The resentment becomes an ambush that lays and waits to attack others, pushing people away; sometimes innocent children, parents, friends or sweetie pie, and like all black hat bad guys, it's the other guy's problem: They are in the wrong place at the wrong time. They shouldn't have said what they said. The ambush worked, we blew of steam and the wounded are bleeding. We drape an invisible cloth of numbness over the mirror so as not to see the pain in the white of our own eyes (Tim Toohey, New Concepts-Ancient Knowledge)

The addict becomes deeply involved in a life style that is unknown to those who do not share the same sub-cultural values, beliefs and language towards the drug. The sub-culture, in contrast, provides warmth and comfort to the addict. Relationships that emerge within this life style are not healthy and supportive relationships, rather they are associates and the glue that holds them together is the drug. It is said that, **"Addicts don't have friends, they take hostages."** They are enmeshed in a world obsessed with obtaining a fix and where one's true value is measured by one's resourcefulness in obtaining a drug. Of course, **there is one consistent friend, that is the love/hate relationship between the addict and the drug.** There are no questions asked, no lectures to sit through: The drug is there when one goes to sleep, and when one wakes up.

The addict may continue to rationalize his real position and feelings. He is convinced that most of the time he is getting along quite well with people. Deep down, however, there is a sense of isolation. A park bench, an abandoned building or car, a rooftop, a secluded ride in a subway car, underground tunnels or out in the world, **the addict is isolated which can lead to a dark and lonely place which is full of despair and hopelessness.** In the words of one addict: "I was a drop out. I didn't eat because food was not important to me. I didn't socialize, I did not bathe, I did not do anything that normal folks do. My existence was based on sleeping and going to get high."

The spirit is destroyed with our destructive patterns of behavior which leaves us with nothing to live for. Once our spirit is destroyed, there is nothing left but an empty shell: The feeling of isolation can be overwhelming. The response, of course is to use. Using represents a learned and reinforced pattern for survival.

> Substance abuse is no longer an option as breathing is not an option. Both are needed for continued survival. Isolation is a survival adaption and we retreat into a shell. Isolation is the body armor. It is bullet proof except when leaving its safe confines in order to fulfill our need. Isolation is a double edge sword. Nothing gets in and conversely nothing is able to leave. The addict becomes a prisoner to the isolation.

Isolation is the soul calling out to the world "help," the mind prisoner, the body slave: the spirit broken, the soul dying; disappear, fading away, the stars to nowhere leading to nothing, a collapsing universe provides structure to receiving those who are falling and those who have fallen.
(Author Unknown)

Chapter Eight

TO THE ADDICT I HEARD YOU

I heard you when you told me that superficial, suave, confident, cool façade was really a mask that you hide behind, that beneath lies a fragile, afraid and alone individual who fears rejection.

I heard you when you said, that a long conviction of worthlessness, have built strong, self contained walls that imprison you.

I heard what you long for: Firm but gentle hands, sensitivity, acceptance and love.

I heard you when you said, you felt different than everyone else, and you had to protect your image when all along wanting to be recognized.

I heard you when you said that all of those years of "crap" in your life, left you with low self esteem, and from a very early age, you felt like you would never go anywhere.

I also heard you when you said, that drugs gave you a sense of security, made you feel warm, feel good. They gave you the sense of confidence that you could take on the world.

I heard you loud and clear when you said, that in using drugs, you had found God: You had found Nirvana.

I heard you when you said, that the powerlessness of addiction, was like falling down a deep hole, over and over again, even though you knew the hole was there. Using became an uncontrollable habit.

I heard you when you struggled with yourself asking: Why do I keep yearning for it, why do I want to keep going back to it?

I felt the powerlessness when you were sitting in the shooting gallery, 7 ½ months pregnant, crying: Why can't I stop myself? Why can't I control myself? I don't want my baby to be born on drugs.

And out of that powerlessness came using, followed by that feeling of security, warmth, and a supreme need to survive.

But I also heard your cries as you walked home after copping. You told me that you kept crying, but I know when you used, those tears stopped, just for a minute anyway.

I heard you when you said that initially using was a fun thing to do, a recreational habit.

But somewhere down the line, you lost all points of reality. You said that people would tell you when something was wrong, but you didn't listen, and somewhere you crossed the line, and all you knew was that you had to use.

I heard you when you tried to play with your addiction, thinking you were greater than it, first moderation, but of course that didn't work. You even spoke of how you refrained from drinking in one bar, only to go down the street and get drunk in another.

I saw your feeble attempts at controlling your addiction, taking ups when doing downs and downs when doing ups.

I saw when the drug consumed you, as you described it taking over your brain, your mouth, and your body, and yet you continued to use, even after being miserable, with no food and no money.

And again, I heard you loud and clear when you cried out to God: I'm caught up in this cycle: How will I get off? You said, that was when it really set in, and that you had crossed the line, but did you stop? No, you were powerless.

I heard you say that from the very beginning you were in denial, that you deceived yourself into thinking, that 40 oz of beer and a left over joint for breakfast was normal.

And I heard you spill one misconception after another: There was nothing wrong with skipping school in the 10th grade, with your friends to get high, that a broken lock and your need for money for drugs justified burglary of a neighbor, who conveniently happened to be on vacation.

I heard you minimize the destructive path of slow destruction taken by you and your associates.

I heard the illusion of control when you thought you could drive under the influence. And if that wasn't enough, I heard the assertion that it was the parked car, sitting too far out in the road that caused the accident.

I heard how you intellectualized the accuracy of the breathalyzer test, and the further absurdity that somehow the officer could not smell the alcohol that emanated from your breath.

I heard your assertion that the reason you drank was because everyone in your family drank, and that the reason you avoided everyone was so they wouldn't know the severity of your drinking, even though they knew.

I heard you when you psyched yourself up to believing everything was ok, even though it wasn't, but you didn't know because you didn't even know you were lying.

I heard you when you said you were angry at all those people who had made your life a living hell.

I heard you when you were mad because no one would hire you, so you kept on drinking, and you felt like a failure.

I heard you when you said you were "pissed off", and felt violated, when everyone asked you to stop using drugs. You said it was your choice and you felt like a second class citizen.

I heard you when you said the pain in your head was so real, it was like a little person who screamed louder and louder to the point you just wanted to cut him out and destroy him,
just to get a minute of peace, just to feel better.

I heard you when you said you felt bad and guilty about everything, and you just wanted to anesthetize those feelings and live a normal life.

I heard you beat yourself up and question why you continued to do the same thing, and asked, what was wrong with me?

I heard how depressed and worthless and disappointed you were in yourself when you came down from using drugs.

I heard your cries.

I heard you when you said you used only because you just wanted to feel good, and what made things worse after feeling good for the moment, the drug wore off, and you fell into a deeper depression.

I heard your desperation when you went from one drug to the promise of relief from another drug.

And again, I heard you loud and clear when you said, Please God, just let me die.

I cried at the vision of you being wet, dark, alone and naked in a closet.

I heard you when you said, that the feelings of rejection subjected you to the shadow where using took you a million miles away, and that hidden in the shadows, you felt
more connected by yourself.

I heard you when you said your very existence disassociated you from your associates which was fuel for mass isolation.

I heard you when you said that isolation was a retreat of some sort, again an illusion of control with the inevitable consequence of detaching from self.

I heard you say that your alienation from people is an ambush that lurks and waits, and pushes everyone who is someone away to becoming victims in a wrong place, at a wrong time.

Ultimately in the end, you are hurt, so you drape yourself with an invisible cloth of numbness.

I heard you say that in the end, you didn't eat, you didn't socialize and you didn't bathe.

You dropped out and minimized to an existence of living to use, and using to live. Using was no longer an option.

I heard you when you said that Isolation was a bullet proof armor, but at the same time a double edged sword because in the end, you became a prisoner to the isolation, and ultimately, that place provided structure for a collapsing universe which received those who are falling and those who have fallen.

Chapter Nine

Now Hear ME

I heard, I stopped, and I listened to you.

You said you were God's child, but did you truly believe it?

You said you wanted respect, but did you respect yourself?

You said you wanted sensitivity, acceptance and love: Did you accept and love yourself unconditionally?

You can't get what you can't give: Embrace yourself.

I can't tell you I understand your pain, and powerlessness, and worthlessness, and low self esteem, and guilt, and disappointment.

But I can tell you that I understand pain, and worthlessness, and low self esteem, and guilt, and disappointment.

I can tell you that I too, am fragile and sometimes it's easier to hide in the shadows.

But far too much time has been spent in that perpetual falling universe.

I extend my gentle hands out to you, I embrace you, and just for a moment in time, I can be patient and tolerant with you, and I can love you until you can love yourself.

Need I remind you, that you are God's child? You may have burned many bridges and many lights have been extinguished because of you, but the God of your understanding shines a light greater than all others, that in spite of you, cannot be extinguished. Raise your head up and look to the heavens. Somewhere you will find the North Star. Let it guide your journey home. Like Moses' exodus from Egypt, your journey will be hard but your faith will see you through.

There is a force far greater than you and He/She heard you when you cried out. He/She was there when you popped that vein and when you took a hit of that pipe. He/She was there when you tripped to a higher level of consciousness and thought you had found Him/Her. He/She heard you when you cried out, "How will I get off this cycle, God, I am caught up," and He/She heard your desperate plea, "Please let me die."

But God has a greater plan for you. You see, you are really not in charge. All of the drugs and all of the time you spent trying to forget or trying to just numb your despair, was just an illusion.

I can't tell you what is going to lead you from your path of destruction, but I can tell you this.

When you said you felt different from everyone else, you are.

When you said you were powerless over your addiction, that was your first step.

Pause, stop the insanity, and reflect on your life. Understand that your life has become totally unmanageable. Look at the destruction and harm you have inflicted on yourself and on others. It's about getting honest.

Insanity is doing the same thing and expecting a different result. So now it is about being open to something new. You asked people to listen to you, now you listen and be open to others' suggestions.

Your road will wind, your path will be clouded with self doubt and self incrimination.

There will be times you may stumble and fall and other times when using may seem to be the easiest route, but your willingness and courage to make it will guide you through the paths of all that is good, and like a Phoenix, rising from the ashes, you will survive beyond your wildest dreams because, you are God's child.

Chapter Ten

To the Skeptics

Does the sight of me still disgust you? When you pass me by on the street corner of any street, when you sit next to me on the train, when you are walking up the stairs of your house, in your neighborhood, and you see me, do you still have disdain for me?

Did you hear me? Were you not listening with an open mind? Do you still judge me? Is it still difficult for you to have compassion for me? Do you still believe that I, like you are not God's child?

Then with all due respect, can you turn to the beginning of this text, and read it again?

If you did not understand me from my heart, maybe if we kick it up a notch and intellectualize a bit, you will understand.

If the "self is the star of every performance, the central figure in every act," then does not my negative self concept and poor self esteem leave me doomed? Was it my fault, that my concept of me was predicated on the short sighted perception of others? If I have internalized an inability to succeed, is it inconceivable that I am not overcome by challenges? When I sought refuge in drugs, those were my alternatives and the reinforcement of pleasure, warmth, and security encouraged my use.

Do you deny, that we live in a "drug oriented, chemically dependent society," where the solutions for all that ails us is in some mind altering substance? Have you never been allured by the promise of relief or a quick fix? How have you really learned to deal with life on life's terms? Do you know that the only real difference between you and me, are the choices we each have made and the imminent consequences that accompany them?

Have you not considered that my powerlessness is not predicated on my weakness, but on the fact that the drug has altered the neurotransmission of chemical substances in my brain resulting in me having a brain disease? Do you not understand that the concept of addiction and powerlessness are inextricably related, that the obsessive compulsive nature of the disease cripples me to the point where I am consumed with using? Have you never felt powerless in your life? You take one step forward and someone, or something, pushes you two steps back. Have you never dropped to your knees, and prayed for strength to get through some tenuous situation?

Do you think that when you asked me, "Don't you see what you are doing to yourself," I didn't? I'm not really blind to the destructive nature of my addiction. Do you understand that denial must thrive, in order for addiction to live? And I go to great lengths using all forms of denial because if I really see the truth, that light will destroy all that is me.

Were you not listening to me when I said there is an intricate web that is spun between addiction and anger: that my anger is my only medium, to feeling alive, in the face of nothingness and deadness?

Do you not understand, that I use because I am depressed, and I'm depressed because I use? I know that you know depression is a progressive disease, and when left untreated, it can lead to suicide. Do you not think that in some small way, the inevitability of what I'm doing has a fatal element to it?

Have you ever been in a room full of people and been the only one there? Have you developed healthy relationships or are you holding people hostage because you are lonely and miserable?

Do you really still think that we are so different?

It's all about choices, opportunities, vision and faith, are you blessed?

God bless us all.

About the Author

Deborah Day Aikens

Deborah Day Aikens has a Ph.D in Criminology with a specialization in Social Control and Deviance. She is licensed and certified by the New York State Social Work Board and the Office of Alcohol and Substance Abuse (OASAS). She has extensive clinical experience which spans over a thirty year period with a focus on addiction and recovery.

Deborah is the former clinical director and presently a clinical consultant for addiction and recovery clinics in the New York area. In addition, she has been a professor at Mercy College and Bronx Community College for twenty years. At Mercy, she is the director of a Certified Alcoholism and Substance Abuse Certification (CASAC) program, under OASAS. She has developed and instructs substance abuse curriculum for both their graduate and undergraduate programs. In addition, she is the Associate Dean for an OASAS CASAC Program at the National Council on Alcoholism and Drug Dependence.

Deborah continuously presents papers educating the public about addiction and recovery.

Her mantra is, "As I live and breathe, I will here and for ever more, champion the struggle and the challenges of addiction as well as the power and miracle of recovery."

Deborah is the author of the book, "The Miseducation of America: There is no Such Thing as a "Crack Head" or a "Dope Fiend."

Made in the USA
Charleston, SC
04 February 2013